Dollars and Cents

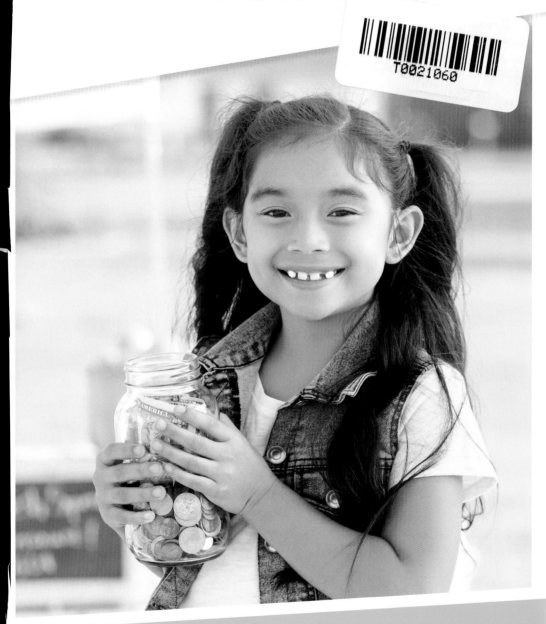

Michelle Jovin, M.A.

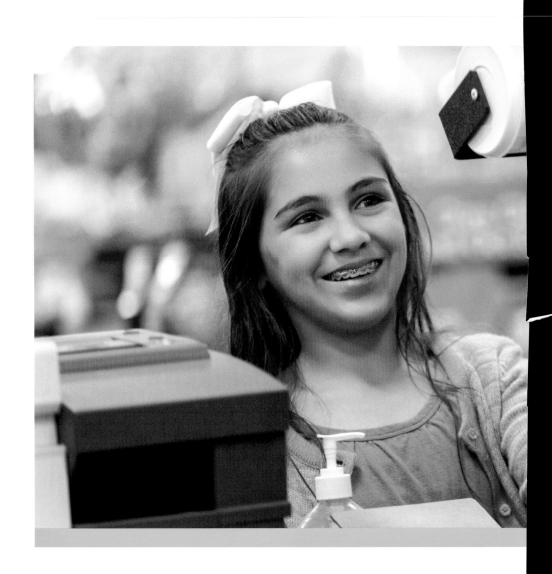

Each country has money.

These are coins.

A penny is worth
1 cent.

A nickel is worth
5 cents.

A dime is worth
10 cents.

A quarter is worth
25 cents.

These are bills.

Think and Talk

What can you buy with a $5 bill?

This bill is worth
1 dollar.

This bill is worth
5 dollars.

This bill is worth
10 dollars.

This bill is worth
20 dollars.

Dollars and cents are the country's money.

Jump into Fiction

Money to Spend

James wants popcorn.

It costs three dollars and ten cents.

He pays with bills and coins.

Now, James has popcorn!

Civics in Action

Some places in a community help others. The places need money to do their work. You can help them get money. You can help them do good.

1. Think of a place that helps others.

2. How can you collect money for this place?

3. Collect the money with an adult. Count the money. Donate it.